ILLUSTRATED BY
CRAIG PHILLIPS

GREAT NATURALISTS

Contents

The Origin of Species	2
Jane Goodall	4
John James Audubon	10
Karl von Frisch	15
Mary Anning	21
Kathleen Drew-Baker	26
David Douglas	28
Naturalists today	30
Glossary and index	32

OXFORD
UNIVERSITY PRESS

The Origin of Species

The Galapagos Islands, September 1835 …

Mr Darwin! Look at this tortoise!

Why, it's so big! I could ride on its back!

Hmm. It looks a *bit* like the ones we saw on the last island, but the shape of its shell is different.

I must remember that …

The Galapagos tortoise is

… You never know, I might need that information one day.

Mr Darwin, I still don't understand. What exactly is a naturalist?

A naturalist is someone who studies nature by **observing** it.

So, can anyone be a naturalist?

Of course! All you need are a few key skills. Come on, I'll show you …

Charles Darwin was one of the greatest naturalists of all time. He wrote a famous book called *The Origin of Species*, which changed scientists' views about how life on Earth evolved.

To be a great naturalist, you'll need to …

… Look.

Listen.

Record.

Identify.

Oww!

Being quiet helps too!

Splash!

Come on … Let's meet some more great naturalists. They might seem very different from each other, but all of them are experts in their field.

Jane Goodall

Jane Goodall has discovered more about chimpanzees than any other naturalist.

"Pop in and collect the eggs, Jane."

Jane started observing animals when she was very young.

"I wonder how a chicken actually lays an egg?"

Squawk!

"Jane, what have you been doing?"

"Oh, just finding things out for myself."

Growing up, Jane longed to visit Africa.

Eventually her dream came true. Aged twenty-six she travelled to the East African country of Tanzania.

Gombe, Tanzania …

There are chimps living nearby, but they run away whenever I get near. How can I get them to trust me?

Lunch is ready!

Of course. Food!

Jane set up an experiment. She waited and waited, and then one day …

At last! I'll call this one David Greybeard.
Stay calm.
No eye contact.
Yes!
Once Jane had won the chimpanzees' trust, she was able to observe them as they went about their daily lives.
She saw that, like humans, they could be kind and gentle …
… and angry and **argumentative**.

Then, one day, she saw a chimp doing something that other naturalists thought only humans could do.

It's David Greybeard.

What is he doing?

Why's he doing that?

SNAP!

Oh, that's clever! He's made himself a tool …

… to catch the termites!

A few months later …

What are they doing now?

They're working together to catch that colobus monkey!

They've learned how to hunt as a group.

Jane's discoveries meant that the Gombe chimpanzees became famous around the world …

… and eventually Jane was able to start raising money to protect the chimps and their homeland.

1934	Jane is born in London on 3rd April.
1935	Her father gives her a toy chimpanzee as a present. She calls it 'Jubilee'.
1952	Jane hasn't enough money to go to university, so she works as a waitress and a secretary.
1960	Jane starts studying chimpanzees at Gombe, in Tanzania.
1964	She marries the film-maker Hugo van Lawick. They have one son – also called Hugo – who spends a lot of time as a baby and a little boy living at Gombe.
1977	Jane starts the Jane Goodall Institute to try and protect chimpanzees around the world.
1980	She is given a special award for Conservation – The Order of the Golden Ark.
Mid 1980s	Jane starts to travel the world to teach as many people as she can about how important it is to save wild animals and their habitats.
1991	She starts Roots and Shoots – a conservation organization for young people around the world.
2002	Jane is honoured as a United Nations Messenger of Peace.
2004	Queen Elizabeth II makes her Dame Jane Goodall.

John James Audubon

London, England, 2010…

The Birds of America by John James Audubon

Sold for £7,321,250!

At the time, *The Birds of America* was the most expensive book ever sold.

200 years earlier … Kentucky, USA, 1810…

The naturalist who created the book, John James Audubon, spent most of his life earning hardly any money at all.

The only thing that really interested him was birds.

Look, Lucy, those are passenger pigeons. There must be thousands of them.

I wonder where they are going?

If we shut the shop for an hour or two, maybe we can find out.

John spent too much time studying birds to be a good shopkeeper.

"H-hem!"

"With you in a minute!"

Before long, he had made over 200 pictures of birds.

But disaster struck …

"Lucy, come quickly!"

"The rats have eaten all my drawings!"

"I can't start all over again."

"Of course you can, John. And this time your pictures will be even better!"

John's wife, Lucy, took a job as a teacher so that John could go searching for birds.

"Good luck!"

"See you in a month or two."

"I must capture how the birds look in the wild."

"Almost finished! Every bird is life-size."

"How was your trip, John?"

"I think we finally have all the drawings we need!"

John had made enough pictures to make a huge book, but no one in America wanted to publish it.

So he went abroad.

Cawwww

I wonder what they will make of my work in Great Britain?

The Royal Institution, Liverpool, 1826 …

No one has ever drawn wild birds like this before.

London, 1827 …

Have we had many orders?

Plenty, and it's rumoured that King George wants a copy too!

John Audubon's book is now one of the most famous natural history books in the world.

The Birds of America
by John James Audubon

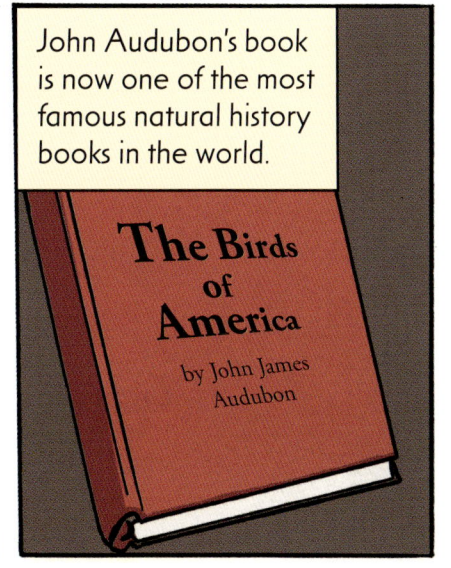

13

John James Audubon facts

1785 John is born in Haiti, in the Caribbean. His mother dies a few months later.

1803 Aged eighteen, John goes to live in America. He starts a business selling food and supplies to the settlers. He teaches himself to draw.

1808 John marries Lucy Bakewell.

1812 John discovers that all his best drawings have been eaten by rats.

1821 Lucy takes a job as a schoolteacher so that John can make more expeditions to observe as many birds as possible.

1826 John completes over 400 life-size drawings of birds. No one will publish them in America so, aged forty-one, he sets sail for Great Britain.

1827 John is a success. His drawings are turned into prints that are sold in sets of five. There are 87 sets. When buyers have collected all the sets they bind them together to make enormous books.

1829–1839 John goes on several expeditions to newly explored parts of America to record the birds that live there.

1842 He publishes a smaller, final, version of *The Birds of America*.

1851 John dies aged 65.

Karl von Frisch

Munich, Germany, 1945 ... World War II has just ended.

If nature can survive, then we can too.

You have much to teach us, my little friend.

Karl von Frisch knew how important bees were. He had studied them for over thirty years.

Bees need flowers; flowers need bees; humans need both!

Bees take **pollen** from flowers to use as food.

In return, the bees **pollinate** the plants, which make the seeds and fruit we eat.

But how do they find the flowers with the best pollen?

15

For a long time scientists couldn't work out how one bee told another bee where to find the flowers with the best pollen and **nectar**.

I have discovered how bees communicate with each other … by dancing!

Rubbish!

Karl had some convincing to do …

Remember, it's usually very dark inside a hive.

So I had a special one made with glass sides.

The bees can't see the dance — they feel it with their **antennae**.

The job of finding the best flowers is taken by what I call 'scout bees'.

Ten metres from the hive …

She's going back in to do her dance.

"The other bees can smell the flowers on the scout bee."

"Round Dance"

The Round Dance tells them the flowers are close by.

"Flowers nearby are easy to find …"

"… but bees often travel several kilometres from the hive."

"She's coming back. This time she'll do another dance."

"Waggle Dance"

"The longer the bee waggles its body, the longer the distance to the flowers."

'1 second of waggle means: "Fly 1000 metres."'

'4 seconds of waggle means: "Fly 4000 metres."'

'Dancing up the honeycomb means: "Fly towards the sun."'

'Dancing downwards means: "Keep the sun behind you."'

'Dancing to the right means: "Keep the sun on your left."'

'The more energy the scout bee puts into her dance, the more pollen or nectar the bees will find at the end of their journey!'

It took a long time for other scientists to realize Karl was right. But, in 1973, he was eventually given the highest award of all … the Nobel Prize in **Physiology**.

Karl von Frisch facts

1886 Karl is born in Vienna, Austria.

1890s As a child, he collects all sorts of living things and studies them closely. He notices the sea creatures he keeps in his aquarium wave their tentacles when he switches the lights on in his room!

1912 Karl works as a lecturer at Munich University, in Germany.

1917 He marries Margarethe Mohr. They have four children.

1919 Karl becomes Professor of Zoology at Munich University. He discovers that bees can tell different flowers by their scent. He also discovers that bees see colours much like humans.

1925 He becomes Director of the Institute of Zoology at Munich University.

1927 Karl writes his famous book *The Dancing Bees* about how bees communicate with each other.

1945 The Institute of Zoology is destroyed in World War II.

1950 The Institute is rebuilt. Karl returns to take charge.

1958 He retires from teaching, but carries on researching animal behaviour.

1973 Karl is awarded the Nobel Prize.

1982 He dies in Munich aged 95.

Mary Anning

10th December 1823, Lyme Regis, England …

Mary Anning was a keen fossil collector and **palaeontologist**.

That looks like the start of another landslide!

That was close. Hang on …

… what's this?!

Clearing away the rock and mud took all night.

This is something new.

21

By morning, Mary had uncovered a complete skeleton! It was the first time an entire fossilized *Plesiosaur* had been found.

Mary's discovery meant naturalists could imagine what this extinct creature might have looked like when it swam in the sea millions of years ago!

Even as a young girl, Mary had been good at spotting fossils.

Keep working, Joseph. The sooner we can move it, the sooner we can sell it!

Mary's father had died when she was only eleven. She couldn't go to school. Every fossil she sold helped keep her family from going hungry.

Thank you ma'am.

Mary kept making new discoveries. In 1828, she became the first person in Britain to find a fossil of *Dimorphodon*, a flying lizard.

Then in 1830 she found another type of *Plesiosaur*.

She even discovered fossilized dinosaur poo!

Mary opened a shop. She had some very grand customers – including the King of Saxony!

Good afternoon, your Majesty.

Today we know Mary was a great naturalist, but back in the nineteenth century things were very different …

23

The Geological Society, London, 1830 …
Women were not allowed to be members of scientific societies or go to university.
The men who bought Mary's fossils rarely mentioned her in their books or lectures.
This new fossil of mine proves my theory …
The Geological Society, London, today …
Mary Anning was one of the greatest …
Things are very different now.
Lyme Regis, Dorset …
You can still find fossils on the beach where Mary used to go fossil collecting … However, there are still landslides, so always make sure you have an adult with you!

Mary Anning facts

1799 Mary is born on 21st May in Lyme Regis, Dorset, England.

1800 Mary, aged fifteen months, survives when lightning strikes a tree under which she is sheltering!

1810 Her father dies and money becomes tight.

1811 Mary and her brother, Joseph, uncover a fossilized *Ichthyosaur*. Mary becomes a full-time fossil hunter.

1823 She discovers the first complete *Plesiosaur*.

1826 Mary opens her shop: 'Anning's Fossil Depot' in Lyme Regis.

1828 She discovers the first British example of *Dimorphodon*.

1829 She discovers a new fossil of a fish, *Squaloraja*.

1830 She discovers a new species of *Plesiosaur*.

1833 Mary is almost buried alive in a landslide that kills her faithful dog, Tray.

1838 The government awards her a small pension.

1844 The King of Saxony visits Mary's shop.

1847 Mary dies in Lyme Regis, aged forty-seven.

Kathleen Drew-Baker

Manchester, England 1949...

Kathleen Drew-Baker was fascinated by...

...seaweed!

It might not sound that exciting, but Kathleen's work helped prevent millions of people from starving...

KNOCK KNOCK

All because something she observed was recorded in a scientific journal.

It's here!

Japan, 1949 ...

"The nori has stopped growing. Soon there will be nothing for us to eat!"

Nori, an edible seaweed, is an important food in Japan.

This might be the answer!

Kathleen had observed that the **spores** of some seaweeds needed old seashells to live in.

Now Japanese scientists knew they had to add old seashells to the seabed to make baby seaweed grow.

"At last! Plenty of food for everyone!"

The people of Japan have never forgotten how Kathleen's work helped them. Every year they hold a festival in her honour.

They even have a **memorial** dedicated to Kathleen.

They call her *The Mother of the Sea*.

David Douglas

The tallest tree in Britain is a Douglas Fir. It is over 66 metres tall.

The timber produced by Sitka Spruce trees is used to make all sorts of things: from roofs to guitars!

Timber from Monterey Pines is used in the construction of houses.

None of these trees had been grown in Britain until David Douglas brought their seeds back from America.

The Fraser River, Canada, June 13th 1833 ...

"Swim for the shore, Billy!"

Plant collecting could be a dangerous business.

David travelled to North America and Hawaii, collecting seeds from plants and flowers.

He introduced hundreds of plants to Britain and was made a fellow of the Geological and Zoological Societies in London for his work.

Naturalists today

In the 21st century, we need naturalists more than ever.

The more people there are on Earth …

… the more we need to study and understand nature.

That way, we can help protect the planet's **biodiversity** for **generations** to come.

"There are no limits to what a naturalist can study."

"So why not give it a go?"

"Remember, the most important skill for any naturalist is to …"

"… never stop looking!"

Glossary

antenna	a long, thin sensory feeler on the head of insects
argumentative	often argues
biodiversity	the variety of plant and animal life in the world or in a particular habitat
generation	a stage in history, which includes people born and living at about the same time
memorial	a statue or structure that reminds people of a person or event
nectar	a sugary fluid made by flowers to attract insects
observing	noticing something and understanding it to be significant
palaeontologist	a scientist concerned with fossils, both animals and plants
physiology	a branch of biology that deals with the functions of living things and their parts
pollen	a fine powdery substance produced by flowers
pollinate	to transfer pollen between plants to allow fertilization
spore	a microscopic cell found in plants

Index

Africa 5–8
America 10
art gallery 13
auctioneering 10
bees 15–19
birds 10–13
Canada 29
chimpanzees 4–8
collecting 21, 22, 29
communication 16
dinosaurs 22–24
discovery 16, 22
fir trees 28
Japan 27
Nobel Prize 19
observation 2, 3, 4, 6
paleontology 21
seaweed 26–27